FOR ORGANS, PIANOS & ELECTRONIC KEYBOARDS

E-Z PLAY TODAY

330

THE NUTCRACKER SUITE

8 Cherished Selections from Tchaikovsky's Ballet

ISBN 978-0-7935-2159-3

HAL•LEONARD®
CORPORATION
7777 W. BLUEMOUND RD. P.O. BOX 13819 MILWAUKEE, WI 53213

Visit Hal Leonard Online at
www.halleonard.com

Overture

Registration 3
Rhythm: March or None

By Pyotr Il'yich Tchaikovsky

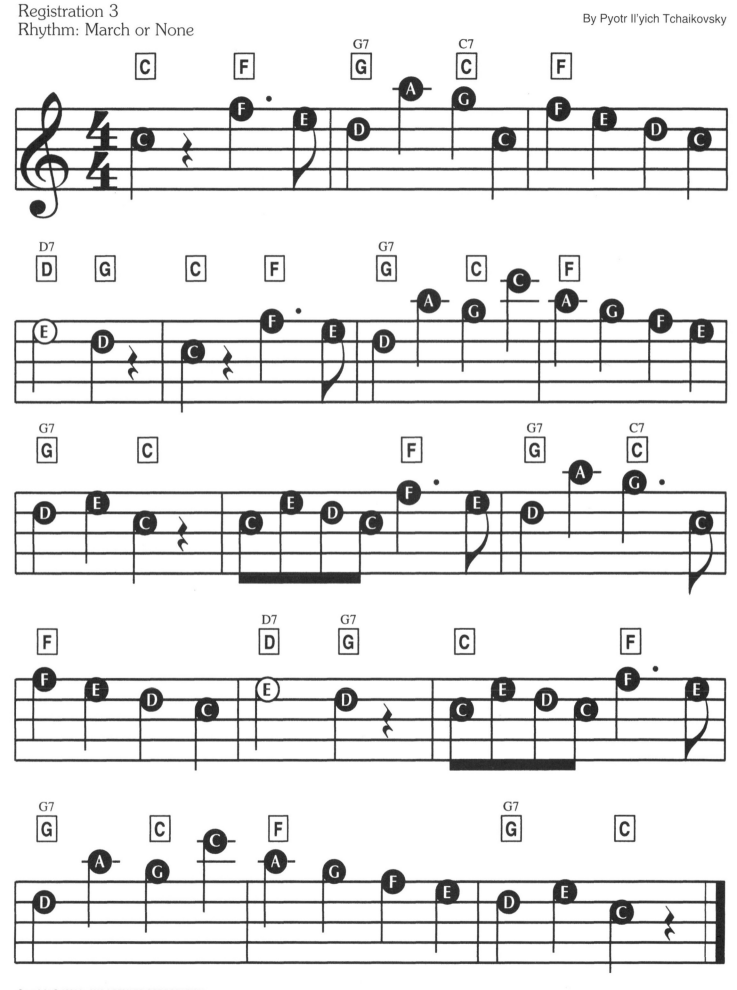

March

Registration 2
Rhythm: March

By Pyotr Il'yich Tchaikovsky

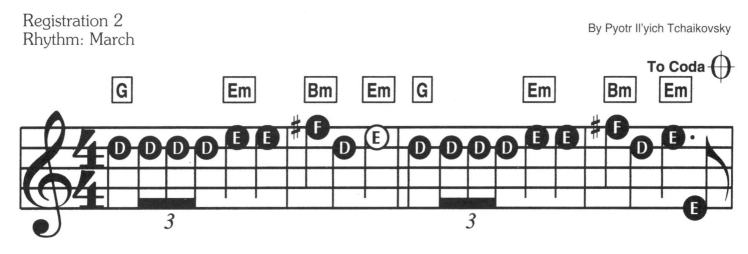

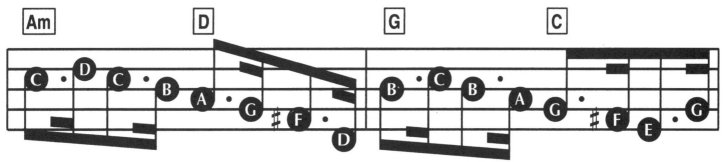

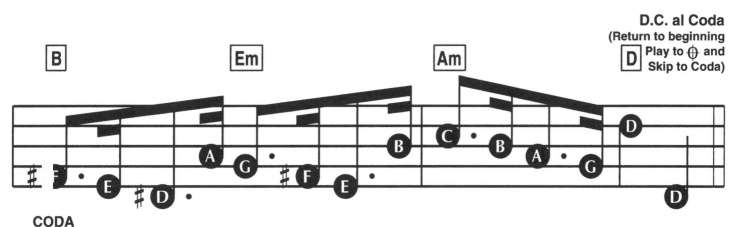

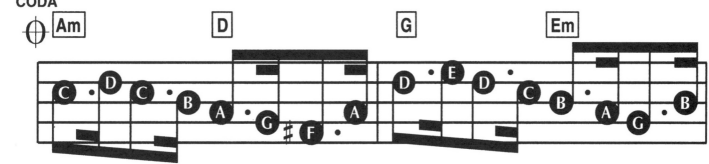

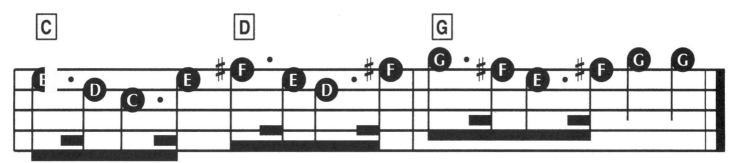

Arab Dance

Registration 3
Rhythm: Waltz

By Pyotr Il'yich Tchaikovsky

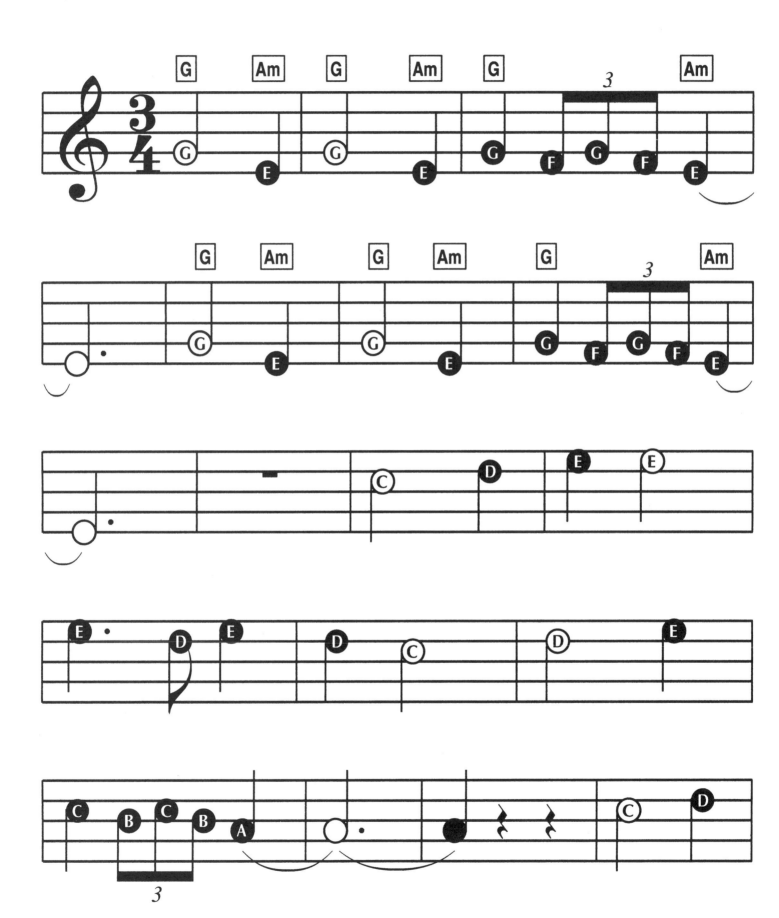

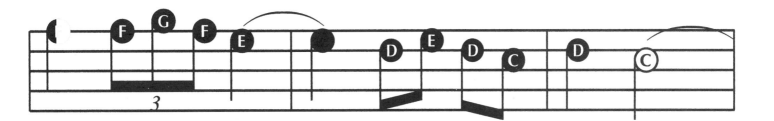

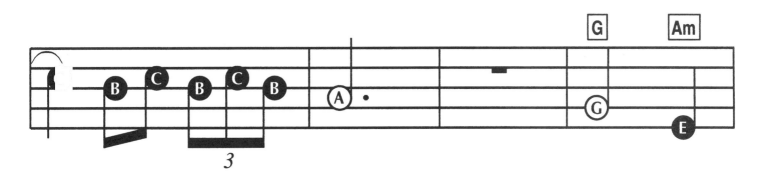

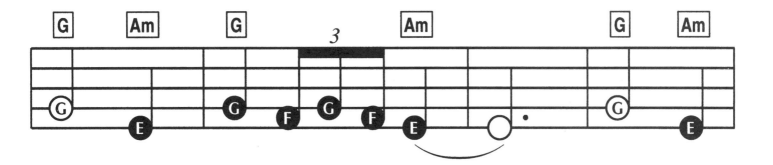

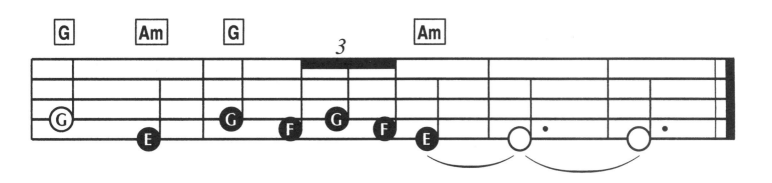

Chinese Dance
("Tea")

Registration 5
Rhythm: March

By Pyotr Il'yich Tchaikovsky

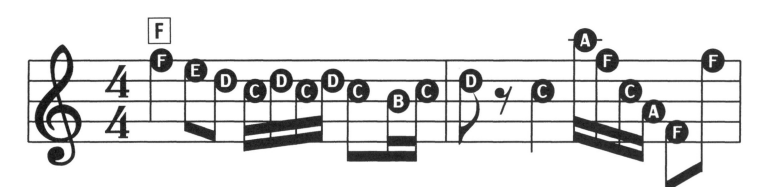

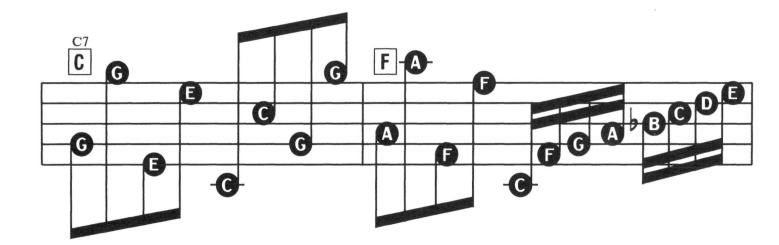

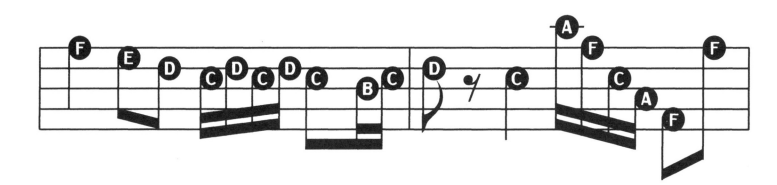

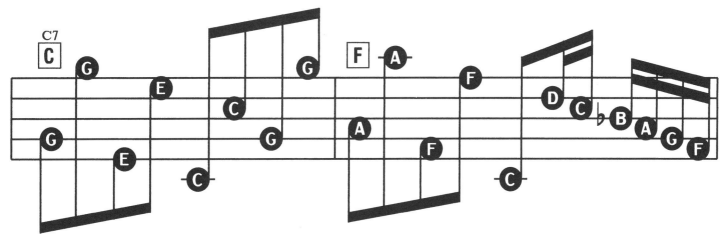

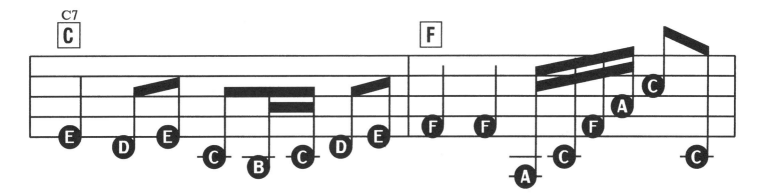

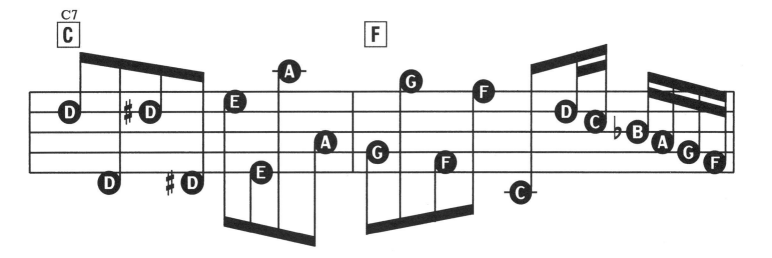

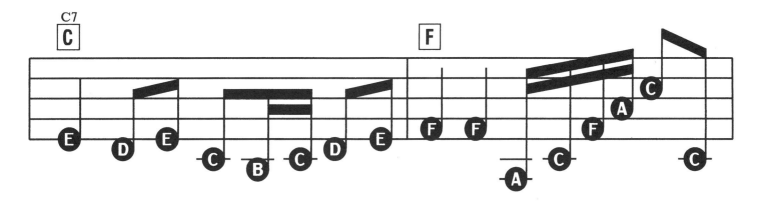

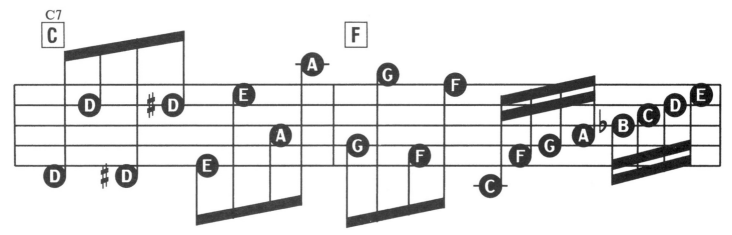

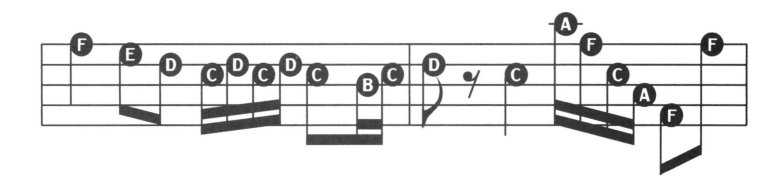

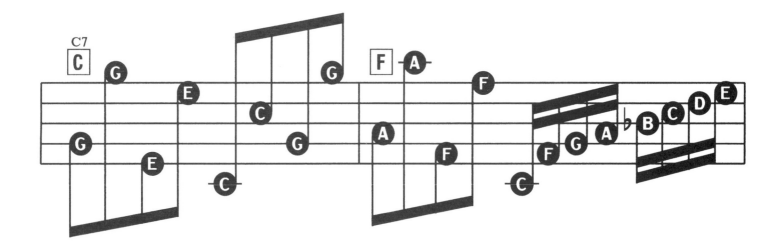

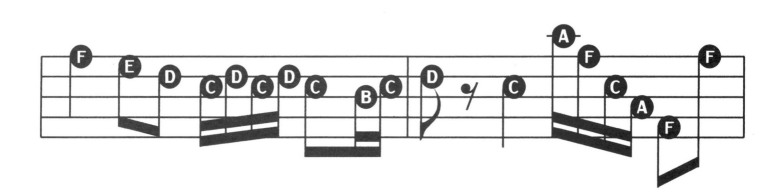

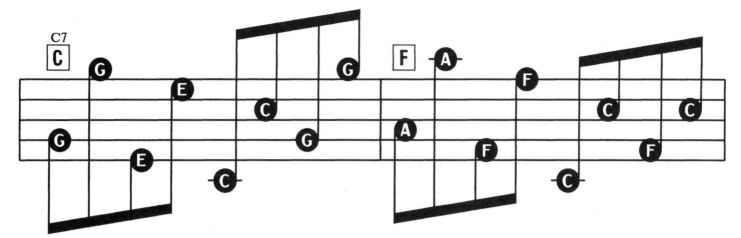

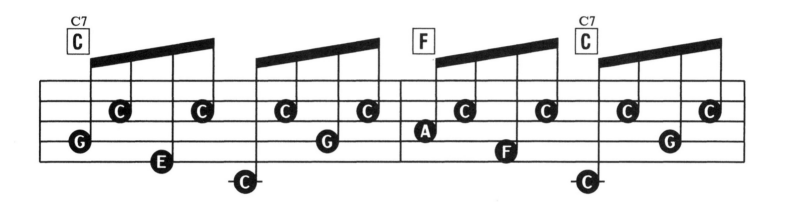

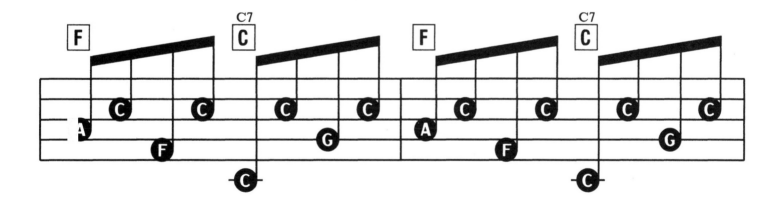

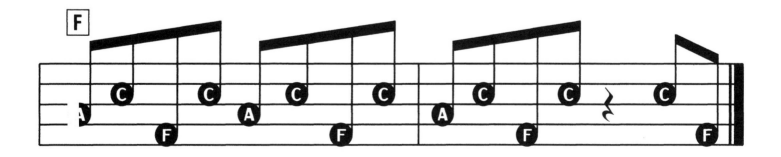

Dance of the Reed-Flutes

Registration 3
Rhythm: March

By Pyotr Il'yich Tchaikovsky

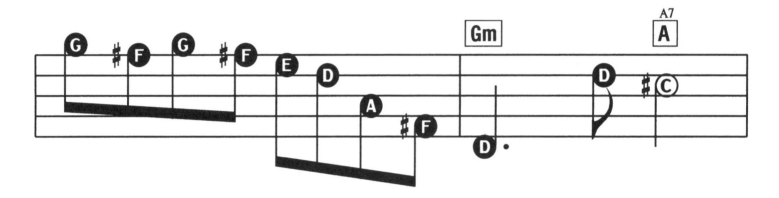

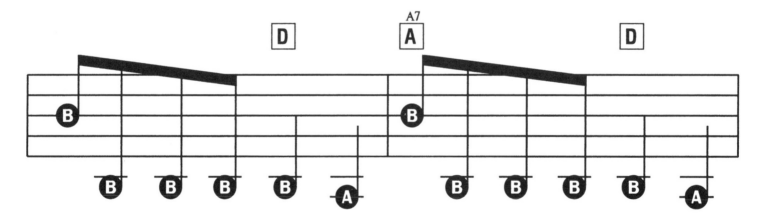

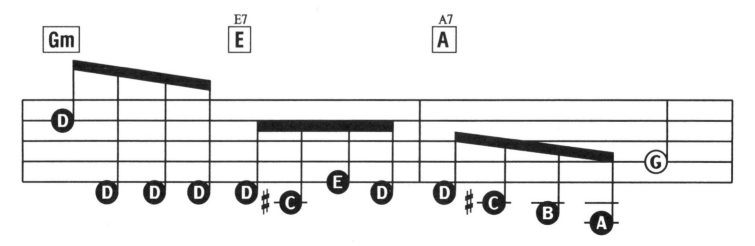

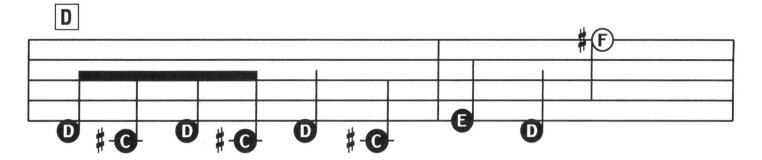

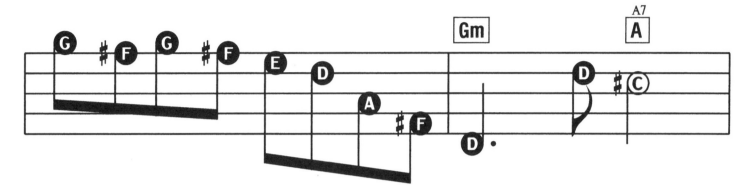

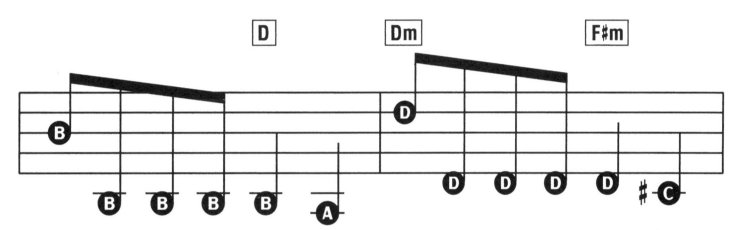

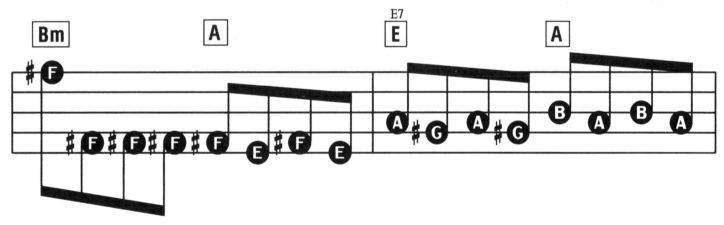

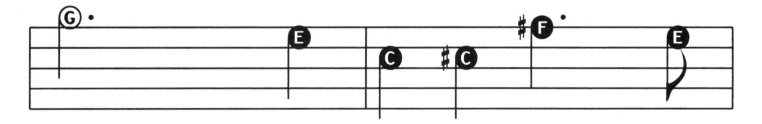

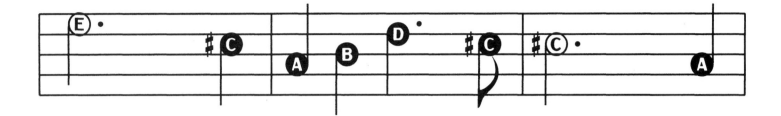

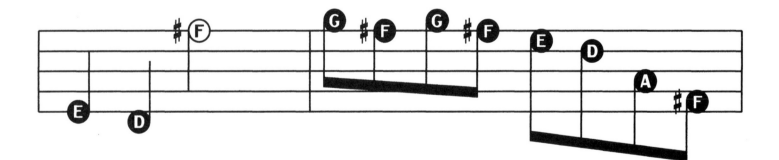

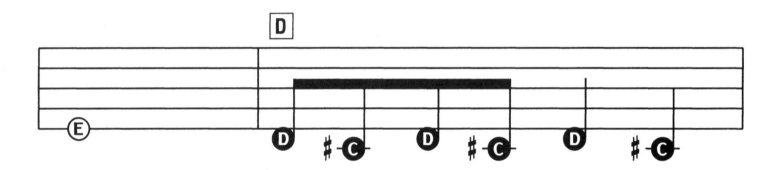

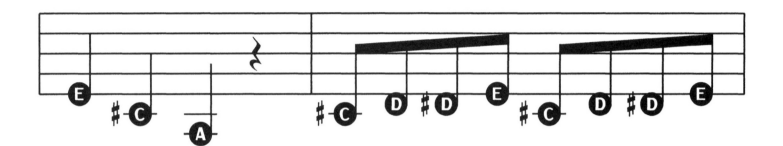

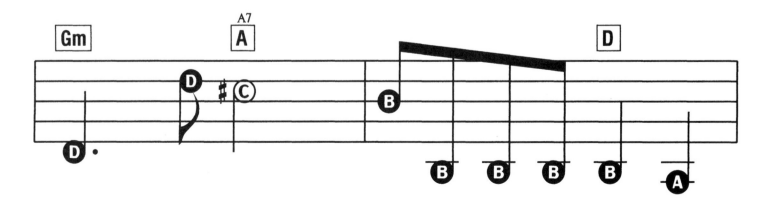

13

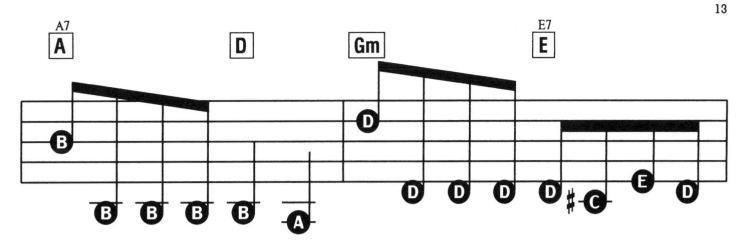

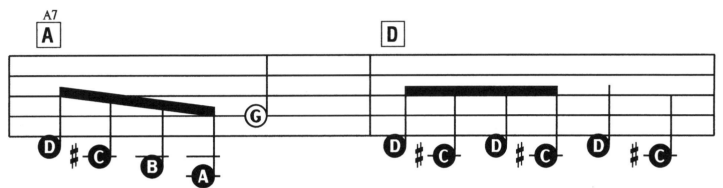

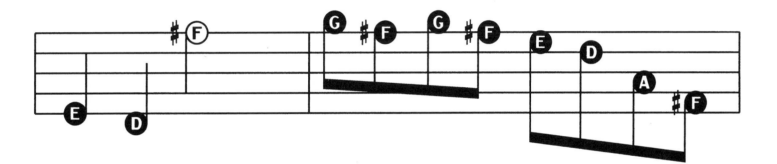

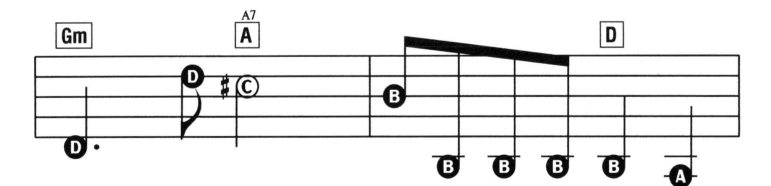

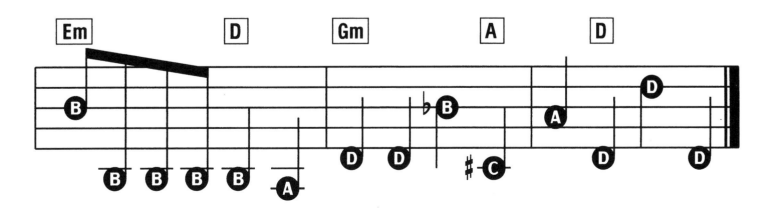

Russian Dance
("Trepak")

Registration 7
Rhythm: March or None

By Pyotr Il'yich Tchaikovsky

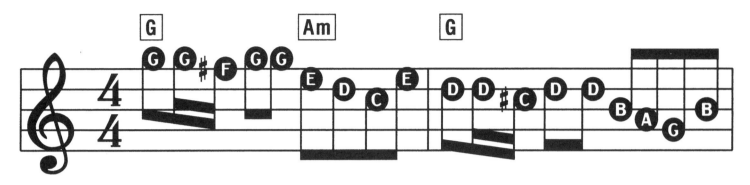

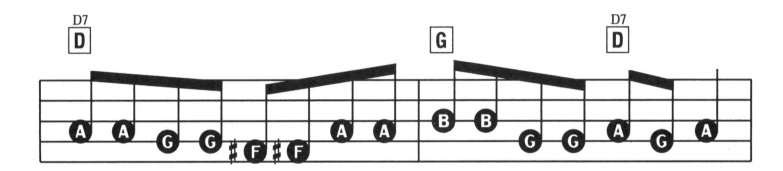

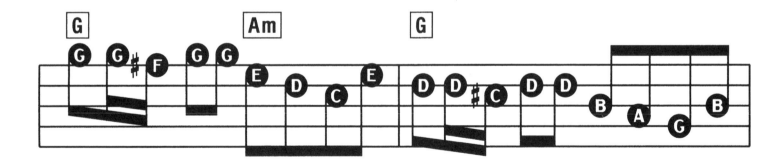

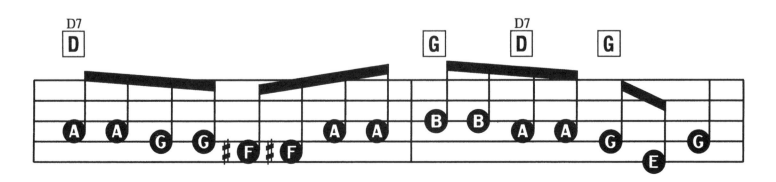

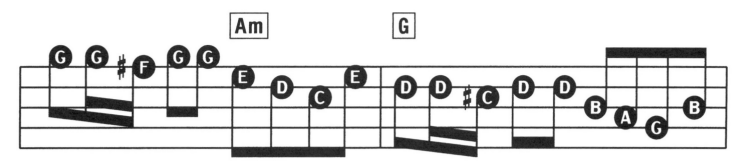

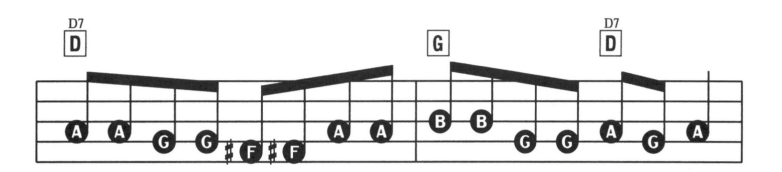

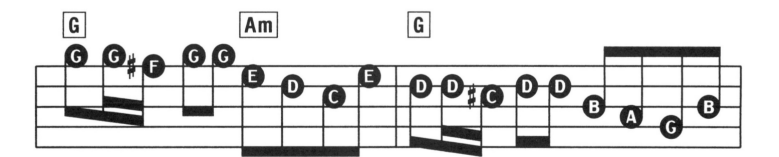

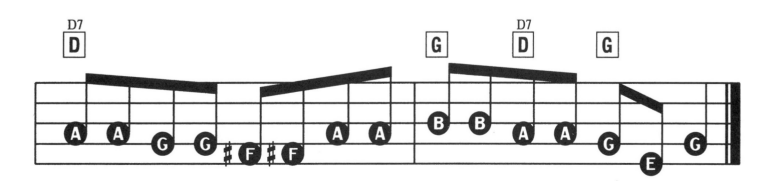

Dance of the Sugar Plum Fairy

Registration 5
Rhythm: March or None

By Pyotr Il'yich Tchaikovsky

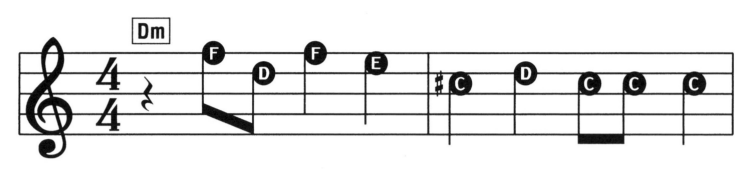

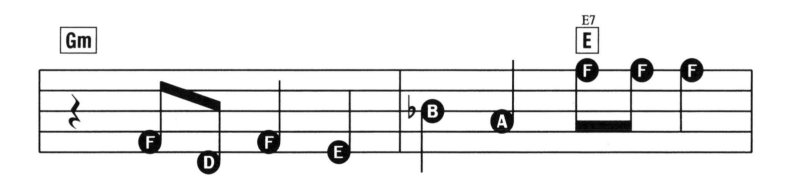

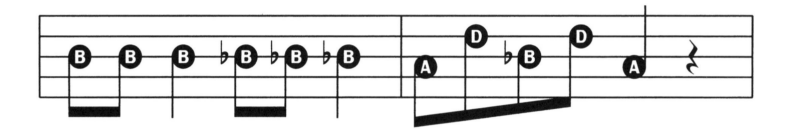

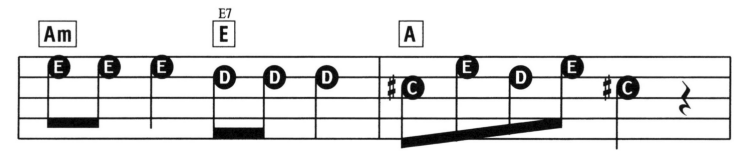

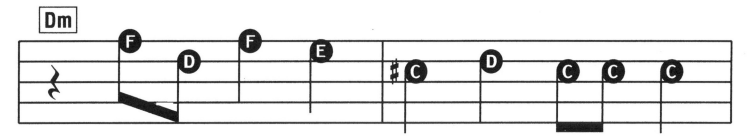

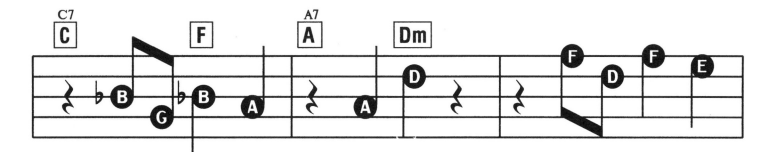

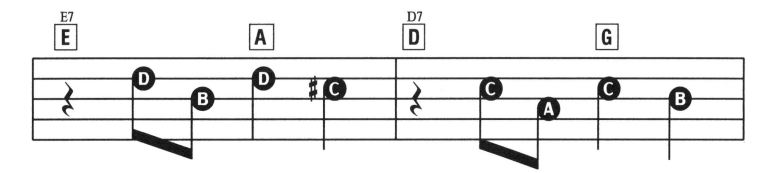

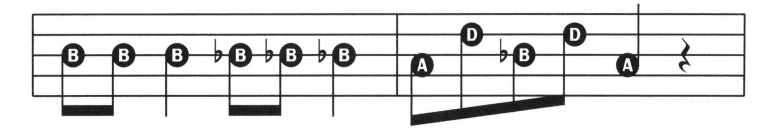

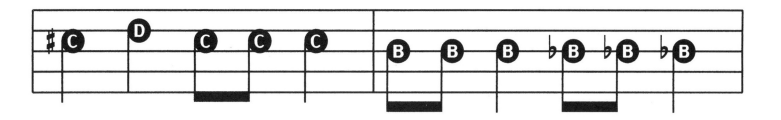

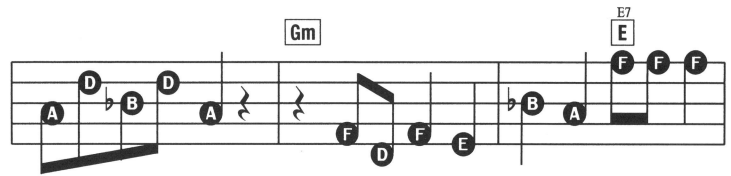

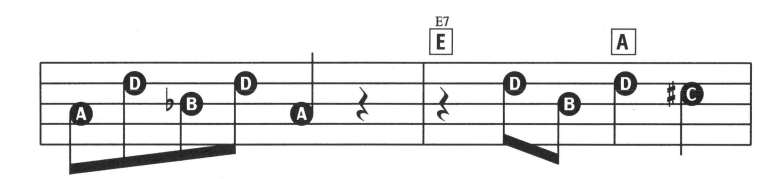

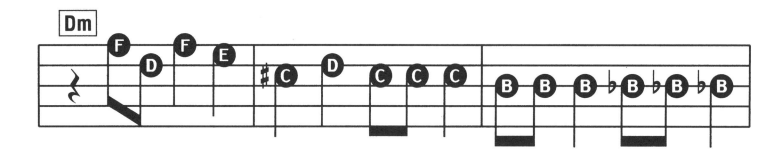

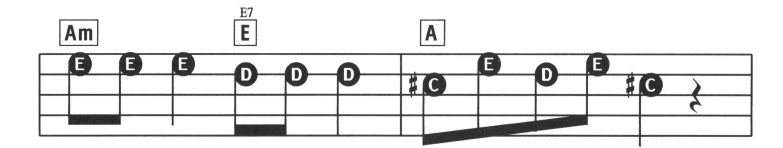

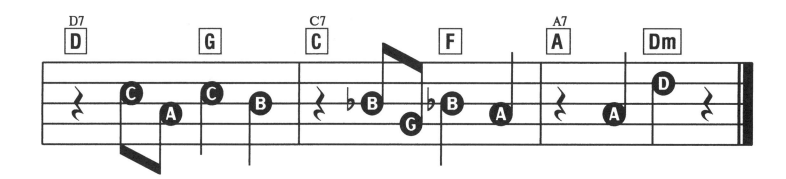

Waltz of the Flowers

Registration 3
Rhythm: Waltz

By Pyotr Il'yich Tchaikovsky

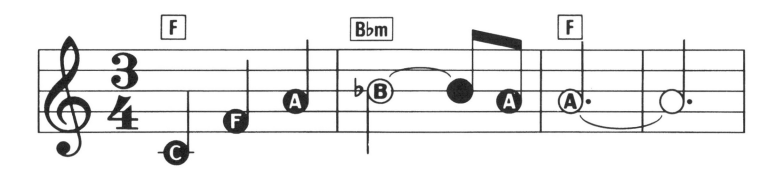

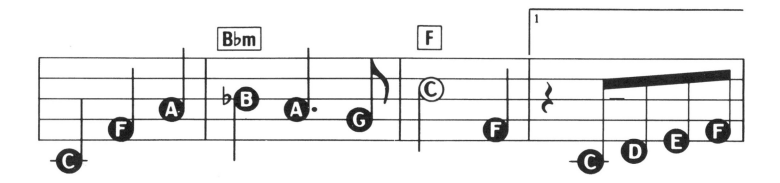

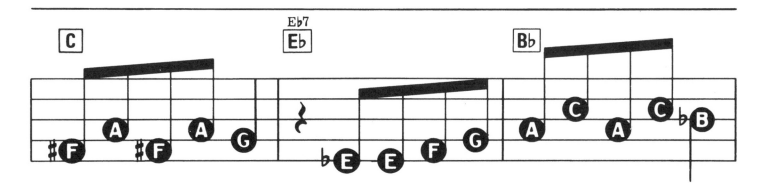

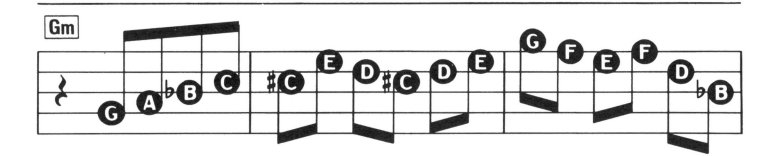

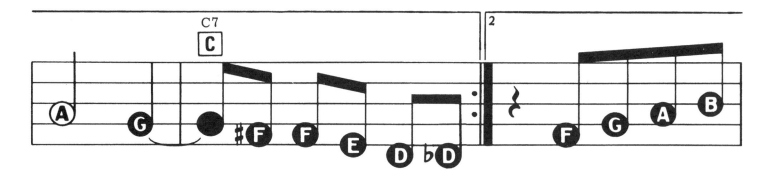

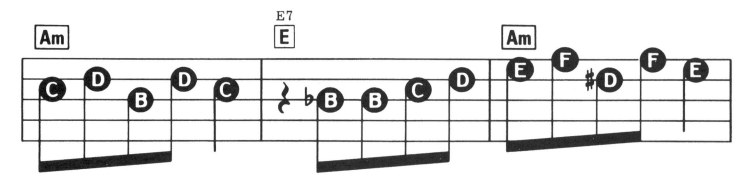

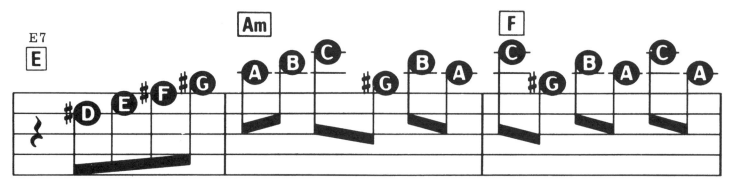

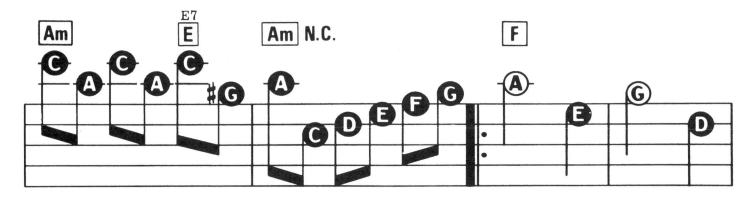

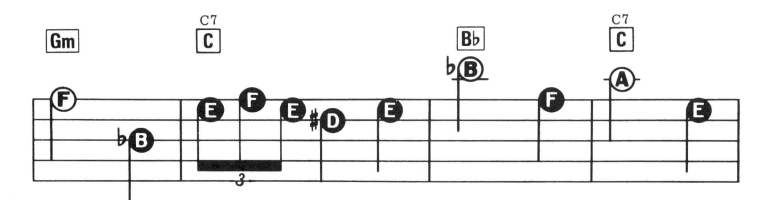

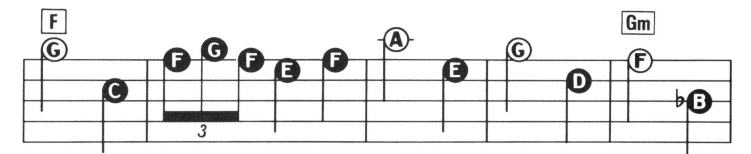

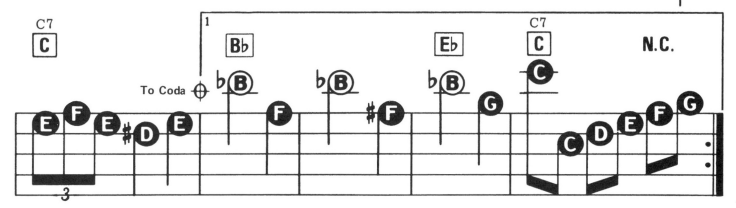

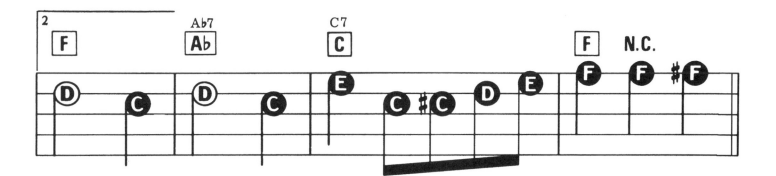

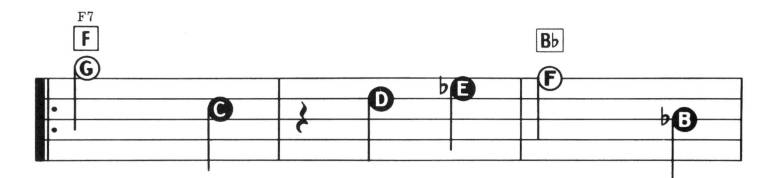

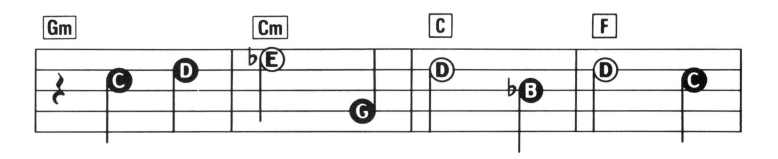

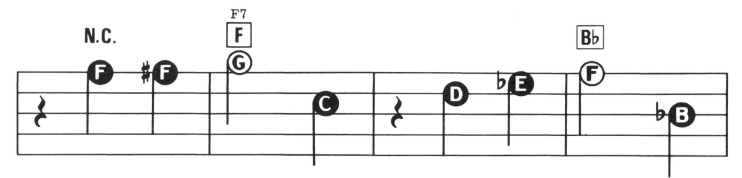

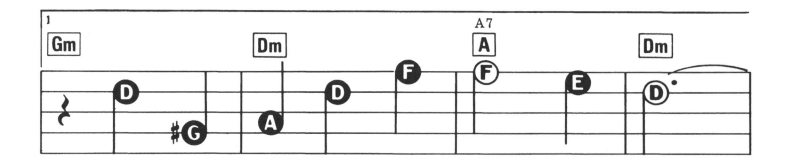

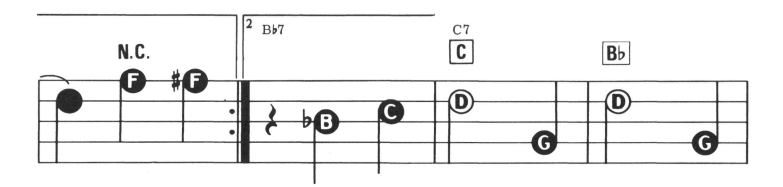

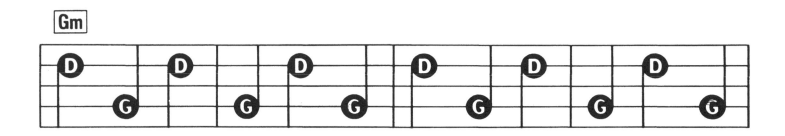

D.C. al Coda
(Return to beginning
Play to ⊕ and skip to Coda)

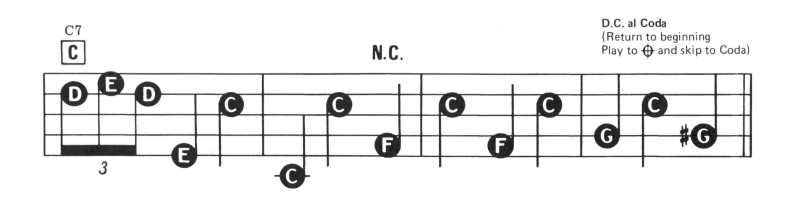

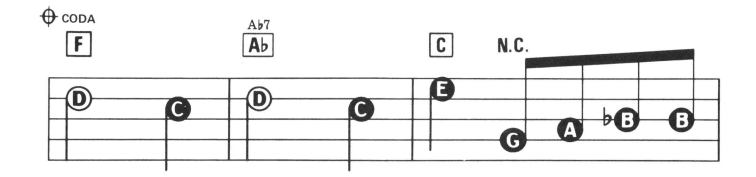

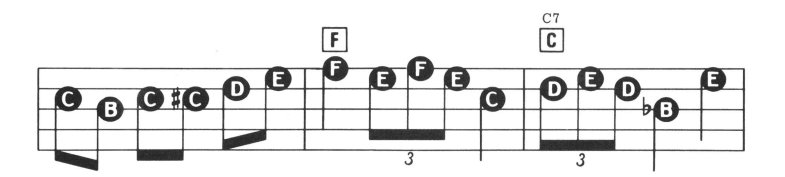

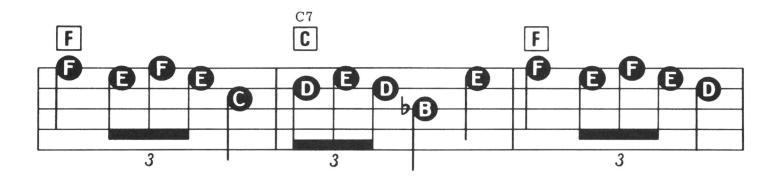

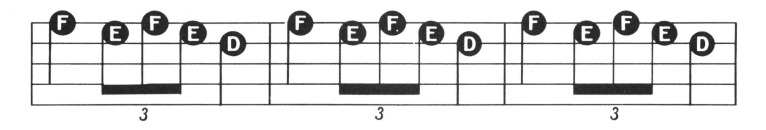

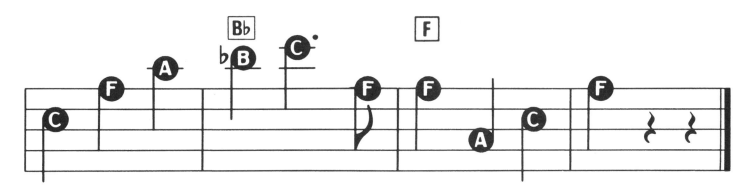

Registration Guide

- Match the Registration number on the song to the corresponding numbered category below. Select and activate an instrumental sound available on your instrument.

- Choose an automatic rhythm appropriate to the mood and style of the song. (Consult your Owner's Guide for proper operation of automatic rhythm features.)

- Adjust the tempo and volume controls to comfortable settings.

Registration

1	Mellow	Flutes, Clarinet, Oboe, Flugel Horn, Trombone, French Horn, Organ Flutes
2	Ensemble	Brass Section, Sax Section, Wind Ensemble, Full Organ, Theater Organ
3	Strings	Violin, Viola, Cello, Fiddle, String Ensemble, Pizzicato, Organ Strings
4	Guitars	Acoustic/Electric Guitars, Banjo, Mandolin, Dulcimer, Ukulele, Hawaiian Guitar
5	Mallets	Vibraphone, Marimba, Xylophone, Steel Drums, Bells, Celesta, Chimes
6	Liturgical	Pipe Organ, Hand Bells, Vocal Ensemble, Choir, Organ Flutes
7	Bright	Saxophones, Trumpet, Mute Trumpet, Synth Leads, Jazz/Gospel Organs
8	Piano	Piano, Electric Piano, Honky Tonk Piano, Harpsichord, Clavi
9	Novelty	Melodic Percussion, Wah Trumpet, Synth, Whistle, Kazoo, Perc. Organ
10	Bellows	Accordion, French Accordion, Mussette, Harmonica, Pump Organ, Bagpipes